Is My Cat a Tiger?

Is My Cat a Tiger?

How Your Pet Compares to Its Wild Cousins

Jenni Bidner

LARK BOOKS

A Division of Sterling Publishing Co., Inc.
New York

Editor:
Joe Rhatigan
Wolf Hoelscher

**Art Director &
Cover Designer:**
Robin Gregory

Editorial Assistance:
Rose McLarney &
Delores Gosnell

Library of Congress Cataloging-in-Publication Data

Bidner, Jenni.
  Is my cat a tiger? : how your pet compares to its wild cousins / Jenni
Bidner. -- 1st ed.
    p. cm.
  Includes index.
  ISBN 1-57990-815-2 (hardcover)
  1. Cats. 2. Felidae. 3. Cats--Behavior. 4. Felidae--Behavior. I.
Title.
  SF442.B53 2006
  636.8--dc22

                          2006023356

10 9 8 7 6 5 4 3 2 1

First Edition

Published by Lark Books, A Division of Sterling Publishing Co., Inc.
387 Park Avenue South, New York, N.Y. 10016

© 2006, Jenni Bidner

Distributed in Canada by Sterling Publishing, c/o Canadian Manda Group, 165 Dufferin Street, Toronto, Ontario, Canada M6K 3H6

Distributed in the United Kingdom by GMC Distribution Services, Castle Place, 166 High Street, Lewes, East Sussex, England BN7 1XU

Distributed in Australia by Capricorn Link (Australia) Pty Ltd., P.O. Box 704, Windsor, NSW 2756 Australia

If you have questions or comments about this book, please contact: Lark Books, 67 Broadway, Asheville, NC 28801 (828) 253-0467

Manufactured in China

ISBN 13: 978-1-57990-815-7
ISBN 10: 1-57990-815-2

For information about custom editions, special sales, and premium and corporate purchases, please contact Sterling Special Sales Department at 800-805-5489 or specialsales@sterlingpub.com.

CONTENTS

You wake up one morning and are walking sleepily toward the kitchen when all of the sudden your pet cat rubs against your leg. She seems cute and friendly, but what your pet is really doing is acting like a wild cat!

Sure, your cat may meow at you once in a while, and you may even meow back for fun. But wouldn't it be great if you could understand what she said? Well, cats only speak words in the movies. However, you can look at your cat's wild cousins (tigers, lions, and more) for hints on figuring out your own pet's behavior. And that's what this book is all about. It will show you how your cat is showing off her wild side every time she sleeps in the bathtub, scratches the furniture, or swats at one of her toys. So, get ready to read about tigers, lions, cheetahs, and even hyenas so you can learn more about your amazing cat.

Cats & Their Cousins

Some of your cat's behavior can be explained by studying her wild "cousins." The domestic cat—your pet cat—has more than 30 wild cousins in the Felidae or Cat Family, such as lions, tigers, and cheetahs. Your cat shares many traits with these much bigger animals, but she's most closely related to the small wildcat, which is just a bit larger (but much stronger) than your cat.

Lioness

Lions live in a group called a pride.

Cheetah

Wildcat

Cheetahs are much smaller than lions and tigers and weigh about 100 pounds. They use their tremendous speed to chase down prey.

Mountain Lion

Few animals have as many nicknames as the mountain lion found in North America. Depending on where you live in the United States or Canada, you might call it a cougar, puma, Florida panther, or catamount.

Bobcat

Two other North American wild cats are the bobcat and Canadian lynx. Both have short stubby tails and a ruff of fur on the side of their faces. The quickest way to tell the two cats apart is to look for light coloration on the underside of the tail. Only bobcats have this marking.

Tiger

Tigers are the largest wild feline by far, with the Siberian tiger weighing as much as 600 pounds—or about the weight of 60 house cats combined!

Lynx

Some Other *Wild* Relatives

Ocelot

The ocelot has an especially beautiful coat. The ocelot was hunted almost to extinction so that people could buy clothing and furniture made from its fur.

Margay

Margays are so good at climbing that this kitten may grow up to spend more of its life in the trees than on the ground.

Léopard

Leopards are very fast and strong for their size. They are great at climbing trees and swimming.

Snow Leopard

Snow leopards have big feet and long tails that help them keep their balance in snow. They can also wrap their long tails around their faces to help keep warm.

Surprise! More Cat Than Dog

If you've ever seen a hyena at the zoo or on a TV program, you probably think they look a lot like dogs or wolves. They even live in packs like wolves. But scientists have proven that hyenas are actually much closer relatives of cats than dogs.

The meerkat, civet, and mongoose are distantly related to the domestic cat.

Hyena

Domestic Cat

Meerkat

The Modern Cat

Many thousands of years ago, wildcats probably came close to humans because they found yummy mice and rats to eat near the places farmers stored their crops. People wanted to protect valuable stored food from being stolen, so they thought highly of the cats that killed the mice and rats. Gradually, the cat became domesticated, or tame enough to live with humans. The ancient Egyptians were known to have worked out a rodent-eating arrangement with the African wildcat, an animal that looks a lot like a modern house cat but is now very rare. It is only in relatively recent years that cats have become pets that are not expected to hunt for a living.

Cat Breeds

Today, there are dozens of "official" breeds of cats, each with its own coat and color variations, and mixed breeds as well. Cats don't vary as much in size as dogs, but they certainly have several different looks.

Domestic cats can have long or short hair, or may even be relatively hairless.

Longhair

Shorthair

Hairless

Rex varieties have interesting curly coats. Their ears can be huge like the Siamese cat's, or folded down like the Scottish fold's.

Orange Tabby

Many cats are solid black or white or have striped, tabby patterns like a wildcat. Bicol-

Tortoiseshell

ored cats have two main colors, while calicos have three or more. Point colored cats have a darker color at certain points of their body, such as the face, ear tips, and tail. And it's no surprise that a tortoiseshell cat looks like a tortoiseshell!

Bicolored Rex (Curly hair)

Breeds of cats don't just look different—they behave differently. For example, Siamese cats tend to be very vocal, active, and friendly. The longhair Persian cat has a more relaxed personality and is much quieter. The Ragdoll is often

a mellow house cat that is quite affectionate with people. Maine coon cats aren't as likely to crawl into your lap, but they're excellent hunters and even swimmers.

Does your cat have a distinct personality? How would you describe it?

Solid black

Point

Calico

Wild Is *Wild*

You may see trained tigers and lions in a circus or other show, but don't be fooled into thinking they are gentle. They are still wild animals. They have just been taught to *act* tame in certain situations.

Any good wild animal handler will tell you that even hand-raised tigers, lions, jaguars, lynx, and other wild cats are quite dangerous.

Some people think it is cool to have a tiger or lynx or even bobcat as a pet. They think that love and care will turn these animals into tame kitty cats. However, they will always be wild, no matter how used to people they are. When the cute cubs and kittens grow up and become more than their owners can handle, wild cats are often made to live in small lonely cages or turned over to a rescue center or zoo.

The tame nature of your pet cat has more to do with thousands of generations of domestication (living with people) than with one or two generations of hand raising. Certainly, the early training and care of a kitten can often make a cat more sociable and friendly as an adult. But a cat living away from people because it was lost or abandoned is still a domesticated cat, not a wild cat.

Can Cats Be Trained?

It's easier to train a dog than a cat because dogs are pack animals, meaning they live in a group with leaders and followers. Dogs usually think of people as their leaders and are anxious to please you.

Pet cats are more independent. They might live in a group in your house, but they are far more self-reliant than dogs. For this reason they are harder to train than dogs, and harder to teach to do a trick reliably.

Some cats can be trained to walk on a leash outside, but it is not nearly as easy to do as with a dog.

But, you can still do it. The secret is to reward your cat. After all, she's probably already "trained" to come running when she hears a can of cat food being opened. If you use food as a reward, you can probably teach your cat to come when called, jump onto a chair or platform, "dance" on her hind legs, or even jump into your arms.

Using food as a reward is the key to training your cat.

The Hunters

Did you know that the sweet kitty that sleeps at the end of your bed is a ferocious hunter? All wild species of cats are hunters who kill animals for food. Your cat is also naturally a hunter, though he gets his food from a bag or can. You can find out a lot about your cat by simply thinking about him as a hunter.

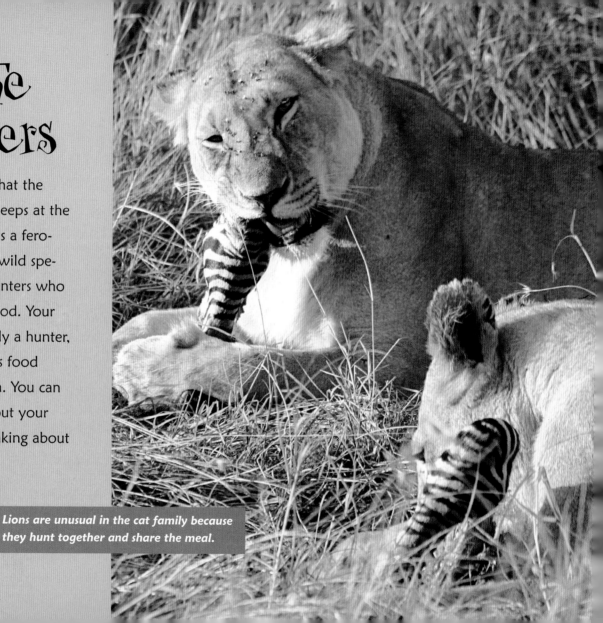

Lions are unusual in the cat family because they hunt together and share the meal.

Big Cats,
Little Cats

The bigger the wild cat, the bigger the game it tends to hunt. Many wild cats can kill animals larger than themselves, but most focus on smaller prey. Lions hunt in a group and can take down a much bigger 800-pound zebra. A relatively tiny pet cat usually sticks to rodents, small birds, and fish if it chooses to hunt.

Hunting *Styles*

Different species of wild cats have developed unique hunting styles based on the food sources available in their habitats. For example, there is a small wild cat in Southeast Asia called the fishing cat that has learned how to scoop fish and other aquatic animals out of the water. Your cat may be able to do this, as well. Cheetahs use speed to hunt down prey. They can run as fast as a car on a highway—more than 55 miles per hour—for short distances. Their great speed and dexterity make them successful hunters. Unfortunately, they are speedsters, not fighters, so they often lose their hard-won food to lions or other predators.

"Leave Me Alone... I'm Hunting!"

Most wild cats are solo hunters. They live alone most of the time, except for during mating season and when the mother is caring for her cubs. Your pet cat would also be a solo hunter if left on her own, unless she found an amazing food source (like a never empty restaurant garbage can) that she might have to share.

Lions are unusual in the cat family because they live in a large group called a *pride* and hunt as a team. Though you might have more than one cat in your house, domesticated cats don't form prides. They're mostly independent animals that might happen to live with other cats in a

person's home. They may have worked out living arrangements with each other, but they won't hunt for food as a group.

Of the wild cats, cheetahs are the next most group-oriented. Cubs will often stay with their mothers for 1½ to 2 years, and older brothers will sometimes band into small groups for a period of time.

Hide & Attack

Most cats use camouflage (see page 29) and stalking techniques to get close enough to surprise and pounce on their prey. You've probably seen your cat do this by crouching low and ever so slowly trying to sneak up on real, imaginary, or toy animals.

Wild cats that climb prefer to ambush their potential meals, often from high ground. The snow leopard that lives near cliffs, the tree climbing margay, and the leopard are among the best ambushers. The athletic serval uses the tactic of surprise, by hiding in tall grass and then leaping high in the air or far to the side to pounce on small animals.

Most homes don't have mice, but cats can become champion fly catchers, or you can amuse them with hunting toys, like a felt mouse tied to an elastic string.

The domestic cat uses all these techniques while playing and hunting. If a kitten's mother brings injured critters to the den to let him practice, the kitten will be a better hunter. But many cats that have never met a mouse can quickly learn some hunting skills.

Day Cat/
Night Cat

Depending on the type of animals they eat, wild cats are daytime, nighttime, or dawn/dusk hunters. Pet cats are traditionally night hunters, which is why you may find your cat awake and active when you're trying to sleep. Cats also have incredible night vision (see page 38), which helps with hunting in the dark.

Your pet cat has probably adjusted to your human lifestyle, but he still looks for hunting opportunities wherever he can find them. Keep fish bowls and bird feeders out of reach!

The Mouse on Your Pillow

Yuck! Imagine waking up to find a dead mouse (or even worse, a dying mouse) next to your pillow. Such a discovery is fairly common for cat owners who have indoor/outdoor cats.

If your cat is a good hunter, she might be able to catch birds or mice and other small rodents. But why does she bring them back to you? She's not trying to gross you out. Because you feed her every day, she probably isn't hungry. But she still has that wild instinct to hunt. She likely thinks she's bringing you a wonderful gift. Maybe it's her mother cat instinct to care for a "kitten," or perhaps she's just sharing extra food with you. Either way, she thinks a mouse on your pillow is a great idea.

Claws, Jaws & Paws

Sure, your cute little kitty doesn't look like a killer, but if you take a closer look at his ears, eyes, claws, and jaws, you'll realize that he's not as harmless or defenseless as he seems. Your cat still has some highly evolved hunting and fighting weapons at his disposal. These physical traits inherited from his untamed ancestors help him survive in the wild and communicate with other cats if he needs to.

An adult male lion has a full mane, while the female lioness does not.

28

Wild Sizes & Colors

Most pet cats are relatively the same size—generally between 6 and 14 pounds and about 18 to 20 inches long from the nose to the base of the tail. However, wild cats have all kinds of body sizes and colors because they live in different habitats and hunt different kinds of prey. Within a species, the animals look similar.

Color variations don't matter for pet cats, but they can be the difference between life and death for wild cats. Stripes, spots, and colors help cats hunt and hide. Both leopard and jaguar spots mimic the dappled sunlight through trees. The snow leopard has white coloration next to its spots because it lives in a snowy climate.

A tiger's stripes blend in well with tall grassland. And the African lion's brown coat makes it harder to see the cat against the brown grass and earth of the plains.

Lions blend in with the brown grasslands.

Leopards and jaguars can be almost black, although this is rare. Cats with this color variation are sometimes called black panthers.

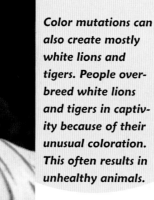

Color mutations can also create mostly white lions and tigers. People overbreed white lions and tigers in captivity because of their unusual coloration. This often results in unhealthy animals.

Cheetah cubs have long hair that sticks up to make them look bigger, as well as to help them hide in spiky grassland.

Leopard:
Solid spots and rosettes (circle-like outlines)

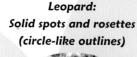

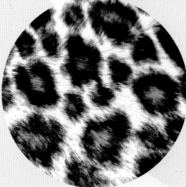

Spot the Spots!

Jaguar:
Solid spots and rosettes with a dot in the middle

Cheetah:
Small solid spots

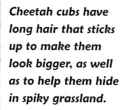

Hear This!

Regardless of how big their ears are, cats have much better hearing than people. They can hear quieter noises,

as well as higher pitched sounds. So if your cat is ignoring you, it's not because he didn't hear you! Their great sense of hearing can help them while hunting and also keep them away from predators. But that's not all their ears do.

Your cat's ears can tell you a lot about what he's thinking. A relaxed cat usually keeps his ears forward and slightly out. Ears that perk up and rotate forward mean he's interested in something. If your cat's twitching his ears (and there are no flies around), then he's probably agitated. Ears flattened against the head indicate fear (though a Scottish fold's ears always look that way). Watch out when a cat flattens his ears and turns the back furry parts of them to face forward. This animal is ready to fight. Turn the page to see photos of what some wild cats are saying with their ears.

Tigers have white spots on the backs of their ears. So, when they turn them aggressively toward their opponent, the signal is hard to miss!

Aggressive cats like this Scottish wildcat will show the backs of their ears to their opponents. Showing teeth is also a threat, since teeth are fierce weapons.

The ears of the caracal have a long featherlike tuft on the tip. This makes it easy for other caracals to "read" the expressions it makes with its ears (see page 31).

This mountain lion is showing displeasure (either fear or worry) by flattening her ears against her head. Her whiskers are also pulled back and tightly grouped (see page 37).

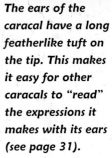

The small serval, with its oversized ears, has more sensitive hearing than most wild cats.

Nosing Around

Cats have a much better smelling capability than people. Wild cats use their sense of smell to hunt animals. They also use their noses to catch the scent of dangers or to figure out if other cats are in the area. The smells other cats leave behind, such as from urine or scent-gland secretions, offer a cat valuable clues. This includes whether the other cat is male or female, if it's interested in having kittens, or even if the cat is healthy or sick.

This lynx smells a tree, probably to check a "scent post" left by another animal.

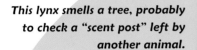

A cat's nose and upper lip are quite sensitive to heat and cold, but surprisingly, a cat's paws and most other parts of the body are not.

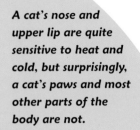

Wolves and many dogs use their incredible sense of smell to hunt. Cats have excellent smelling abilities, too, but they rely more on sight and hearing for hunting.

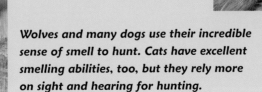

Wacky Whiskers

Speaking of noses, what's up with those whiskers? Well, they're not just for decoration, like a beard. Your dad might shave his whiskers most mornings, but you wouldn't *ever* want to do that to a cat!

Cats have excellent low-light vision (see page 38), but their whiskers can help them travel in pitch-black situations. They use their whiskers to feel the way air bends around nearby objects—so they know something is there without seeing or touching it!

If you watch how your cat positions his whiskers, you can sort of read his thoughts. Fanned out whiskers usually indicate a cat is relaxed. Whiskers held in a tighter formation (scrunched up) and backward may be showing fear. Cats may curl them forward when they're curious or feeling especially bold. Page 32 shows an aggressive wild cat with boldly spaced whiskers. The mountain lion on page 33 has her whiskers pulled back and tightly grouped because she's frightened or worried.

Most cats have the same number of whiskers, but the one on bottom left is more fearful or worried. See how she's scrunched them together?

I See You!

Cats' eyesight is both better *and* worse than humans'. It's better because cats can see in much dimmer light and have a wider view from right to left. It's worse because they don't see colors as well as we do.

Domestic cats are nocturnal (night) hunters, so their eyes are very sensitive to light. In low light, their pupils open very wide to let in as much light as possible. However, when they are in bright sunlight, their slit-shaped pupils get really small to block it out.

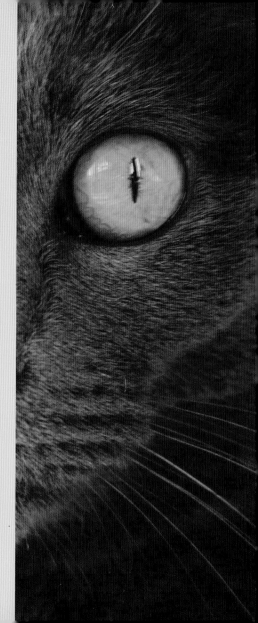

Their slit-shaped pupils are much better than our circular pupils at blocking out light. This is where lions prove themselves to be unusual

Scared or extremely excited cats, like this kitten, will sometimes have very large (called dilated) pupils.

again. They don't have slit-shaped eyes like other cats. Lions probably evolved this way because they are daytime hunters and don't need the extra low-light sensitivity nocturnal cats have.

Some wild cat species are more visually oriented than others. Cheetahs, for example, rely more on keen eyesight when hunting than other cats. They're often compared to greyhound dogs because both animals run down prey with great speed and dexterity.

There is a stone called "Tiger's Eye" because it looks like a cat's or tiger's iris (the colored part of the eye).

Did you know all kittens have blue eyes when they are very young? Their true eye color develops later.

This tiger's tail is straight up for balance as it leaps, and when it is excited.

Telling Tails

Your cat's tail is incredibly important. Just as we use our arms to keep our balance, a cat uses its tail to do the same. Without tails, pet cats and wild cats wouldn't be as good at jumping, falling, or walking along a fence.

Cheetahs use their powerful tails to help them make fast turns at high speeds. Snow leopards use their tails for balance on high cliffs. Tree-climbing wild and domestic cats use tails for balance on limbs. And cats with big furry tails can stay warm by wrapping them around themselves like scarves.

Cats also use their tails for communication. A twitching tail can mean the cat is agitated or having trouble making a decision (such

Your cat may wrap her tail tightly around herself to keep warm in cold weather, or when she's nervous.

When a cat stands on his hind legs, his tail provides counterbalance.

This cat's tail is helping her keep her balance while lying on a narrow railing.

Snow leopards have extremely powerful tails, which help them leap, turn, and maintain balance on high cliffs.

as whether to say "hello" to a stranger or run away). The kitten might hold its tail straight up in the air to make it look bigger to potential predators. Your cat may also greet you with an erect tail, which is the same way a kitten greets its mother.

Oddly, some pet cats, like the manx, have short, stubby tails, as do the bobcat and lynx in the wild.

Powerful Jaws

The secret to the cat family's hunting success is its fast killing ability. Pet cats and all the wild species of cats have extremely powerful jaws.

More importantly, they have the instinct and athletic ability to quickly place a killing bite at the back of their prey's neck. Their whiskers help them place their teeth in the right spot, even in the dark.

If the animal is too big to bite in this way, wild cats usually bite the throat of the animal to suffocate it. Powerful jaws and neck muscles are also important for carrying hard-won (or stolen) meat to a safe place where the cat can eat it or save it for later.

If you have a cat and a dog, you probably think the dog is the better biter. However, pound for pound, most cats

can bite much harder than dogs. Sound impossible? Not if you do the math. If you have a big 80-pound dog like a Labrador retriever, then imagine an 80-pound version of your cat—about 10 times bigger! That much bigger cat would clearly be the winner in a biting contest.

Though house cats are capable of killing and carrying away full-grown rabbits, most are content with baby rabbits, mice, birds, and other small animals.

What a View!

Cats and some of their cousins are good climbers. Most cats have no trouble jumping onto a 5-foot high mantelpiece or to the top of a really tall bookcase. If they go outside, they can easily jump onto a tree and then use their claws to pull themselves upward.

Leopards are well-known climbers. They often drag their dead prey into trees to keep the food safe from other predators that want to steal it.

Cats love high perches because they can watch the world go by. They rarely fear heights, and their balance and athletic ability keep them safe on narrow ledges and high tree limbs.

One of the more amazing aspects of a cat's claws is that they're retractable. This means they can be pulled into the cat's paws for everyday activities and play fighting (see page 50) but are instantly available for climbing, hunting, and serious battles.

Unfortunately, a tree isn't the only thing your cat can climb. Your pet's climbing skills can destroy the screens on your doors and windows, or cause welts on your legs. That's why it's important to provide treelike perches for indoor cats, such as a spot on the bookcase that's reserved just for them.

Hunting Isn't Everything

Sure, cats spend an awful lot of time hunting (even if it's only stalking a dirty sock), but that's not all they do. Cats (wild and mild) have many other traits that are very interesting.

Good Mom!

A mom cat may move her den from the birthing spot to a different location. The new site is probably cleaner, safer, and closer to food sources.

She will carry the kittens, one at a time, by the scruffs of their necks. She also uses this technique to bring back kittens that wander too far away from her. Wild cats care for their young in a similar manner, but there are more dangers for them to deal with, from other animals killing the babies to shortages of food and water.

If it weren't for nurturing and careful moms, kittens and cubs wouldn't have a fighting chance. Why? Cats and their cousins are born helpless. Their eyes are not yet open and they can't hear, so they're entirely dependent on their mothers. At about two weeks old, pet cats open their eyes and start to become more mobile. Mother cats nurse their young and protect them from predators until they're old enough to take care of themselves.

Kittens nurse until they are about seven weeks old. If a young kitten is orphaned, it must be fed by hand unless a foster mother can be found.

A *Sandpaper* Washcloth, Anyone?

Why are dog kisses wet and sloppy, but cat kisses scratchy? It's because cats use their tongues a lot to bathe, and dogs don't do that as much. Cat tongues are rough and barbed, which makes them better grooming tools. It also makes them feel scratchy.

Pet cats and wild cats either use their tongues to groom directly or they lick their paws and wipe their faces, ears, and other areas their tongues can't reach.

Pet cats that live together (or lions in a pride) may groom each other as a social activity and to help with hard-to-reach places. Licking you is a cat's way of being sociable.

Cats groom themselves for many reasons. The most obvious are to keep clean and to keep their coats smooth and even for better insulation. The saliva they spread works similarly to our sweat—it cools the animal through evaporation. Some cats may spend two or three hours just grooming!

You can clearly see the rough texture of this lion's tongue as he opens up and says "Ahhhh."

Because mother cats groom their baby kittens, some adult cats may groom themselves for comfort when they're nervous or uncomfortable. When you pet your cat, she often finds it soothing because it probably feels a little like being groomed by her mother.

The rough texture of cats' tongues may help them gather more water when drinking.

Play Fighting

Cats of all ages will often play fight. Even if it looks like a horrible struggle, it's all for fun because nobody gets hurt. Play fighting can range from a clawless slap with a paw to a rolling wrestling match.

A clawless swat with a paw can be a warning to another cat, or the start to a play-fighting match.

This lion has many scars from real fights using claws and teeth as weapons.

For wild animals, most play fighting occurs when cats are young and learning valuable self-protection and hunting skills. Cubs and "teenage" wild cats practice killing bites to the neck. The lion cub in the photo above swats an older sibling. In a real fight, teeth and jaws are the main weapons—claws are of secondary importance.

When Things Get Serious

Adolescent and adult cats can have real fights as well, especially if you have a lot of cats in your home. Usually, one cat is in charge. He or she gets the best sleeping spaces or the first crack at toys and treats. The more cats you have, the more complicated the power structure and the more likely it is there will be fights.

Are You Ever Going to *Wake Up?*

Cats that grow up together will sometimes nap together, but many cats still prefer to nap alone.

Pet cats, who inspired the phrase "catnap," are also champion nappers. Some cats spend as much as two-thirds of their lives sleeping (16 hours a day, or about twice as much as people!). And, yes, they do dream, but we can only guess what they dream about.

Shhh! It's naptime.

After all that hunting, nurturing, playing, and fighting, it's time for a nap!

When wild cats are not hunting, grooming, or caring for their young, chances are they're sleeping. Hunting takes a lot of energy, so resting is important.

Your Cat's Strange Behavior

There are lots of other things your cat does that can be explained by looking at his wild cousins. Here are a few cool examples.

Why Does My Cat Look Big...

and Small?

When cats are fearful, they often try to make themselves look big and tough, or they try to become tiny and hide. The cat above is arching her back and standing all her hair on end to make herself appear bigger than she actually is. Meanwhile, this kitten (middle) and lion cub (left) are trying to make themselves small and harder to notice.

Looking big and looking small are two good defensive tactics for cats in dangerous situations.

You'll often see tigers at the zoo cooling off in water. If the water is deep enough, they are excellent swimmers.

But wild cats from cold places absolutely hate getting wet because it makes them even colder. Their fur stays wet and can't block out the frigid air. So if your cat cringes at the sight of a filled bathtub, it could just be a natural reaction. However, not all pet cats hate water. Turkish van and Maine coon cats are often excellent swimmers, and many even seem to enjoy getting wet.

If you must bathe your cat, use rewards to make it a less frightening experience.

Why Does My Cat
Hate the Water?

Your cat's not a wimp. Snow leopards, lynx, bobcats, and mountain lions don't like water either.

However, tigers, lions, jaguars, ocelots, and jaguarundi love to swim. This is because they live in hot climates and need to cool down.

A fence railing makes a treelike scratching post for this kitten.

Why Does My Cat
Scratch the Furniture?

Most people think cats scratch furniture to sharpen their claws, and that's part of it. Cats' claws are constantly growing, and they grow in layers. Scratching on the arm of the couch is a good way to remove the old outer layer of their claws and to expose the fresh, sharper claw beneath.

But why do cats sometimes scratch a chair or the couch instead of that cool carpet-covered scratching post you just bought for them? Because scratching is their way of signing their names—in smells!—on important objects in or

at the edge of their territory. They have a lot of scent glands in their paws, and scratching releases these scents. Since you probably spend a lot of time sitting on the couch watching TV, it already smells like you. When your cat claws the couch, it just adds her scent, too.

This snow leopard is clawing a rock to mark its territory with scent.

Why Doesn't My Cat Roar?

Your cat might be able to meow loudly or screech in pain, but it can't make the heart-stopping deep roar of a lion. Too bad, because there are few things as impressive as hearing a regal lion roar.

Surprisingly, lions can roar, but they can't purr. And pet cats can purr, but they can't roar! The two noises require different physical traits, and no cat species can do both.

A few wild cats, like the snow leopard and the clouded leopard, can do neither!

So whenever your cat curls up in your lap and starts purring, know this is her special sound. Air flowing in and out of her throat causes vibrations in her vocal cords and produces the unique sound. Purring is usually an expression of affection, but it can also mean a cat is frightened or agitated.

In addition to a few varieties of the "meow," other common cat noises are a loud cry, a soft mewing greeting, a snakelike warning hiss, a painful shriek, and chattering teeth. Chattering teeth mean a cat is especially excited.

Lions, tigers, leopards, and jaguars can make a roaring noise, but can't purr. Pet cats, cheetahs, mountain lions, and most other wild cats can purr, but not roar.

Why Does My Cat Rub My Legs?

Many cats greet their favorite people by rubbing against their legs. If it doesn't make you trip, it's really cute. Think of it as your cat's way of giving you a warm welcome.

The pictures on this page show two cats greeting each other by rubbing their faces together and two tigers doing the same. Both kinds of cats have scent glands in their faces and cheeks, so they are sharing smells, which is very comforting to them. The behavior probably started when they were kittens, because a kitten will often greet its mother by rubbing against her face.

Of course, you are much taller than your cat, and it can't rub against your face unless you crouch down. Your legs are a good substitute.

Why Does My Cat Sleep in Weird Places?

If you're a cat, places like a sink, a sock drawer, a windowsill, a bookcase shelf, or an old bag or box don't seem like weird places for a nap. They seem comfortable! A ceramic sink is nice and cool on a hot day. The windowsill is nice and sunny on a winter day, which warms the cat and may help him produce vitamin D. The bookcase shelf gives a high view of the world—great for spotting potential prey and dangers. And a sock drawer or a box gives the comforting, snuggly feel of the first den his mother made for him.

Where to Meet Wild Cats

This book shows you many of the ways that house cats and tigers, lions, and other wild cats are similar and different. Your cat has maintained some of its old wild instincts, but gained other characteristics that make her a better member of your family.

A great way to learn about your cat is to start a notebook or journal. Write down all the things you see your cat do. Then compare these notes to what you have learned about cats and their wild relatives in this book.

It's easy to observe your cat or a friend's cat. Seeing lions and tigers and bobcats is a little harder. Native wild cats like bobcats, lynx, and mountain lions usually try to avoid humans, so it's not easy to see them in the wild. That's a good thing, because they're wild. And the quickest way to turn a wild animal into a danger or nuisance is to take away its fear of people by purposefully feeding it or accidentally leaving an unclean campsite.

To meet wild cats in a way that is safe for you and them, visit a zoo or wildlife center.

If you're lucky enough to travel to Africa, you can see lions, cheetahs, and leopards in the wild in the great national parks of Tanzania, Kenya, and South Africa. In the dry season, animals tend to gather around watering holes where they can be safely observed.

Several excellent websites can provide you with more information. For information on cats, visit *www.kidsgowild.com*; *www. kidsplanet.org*; *www.sandiegozoo.org/kids*; *www.animaland.org*; and *www.kids.cfa.org*.

Now that you know more about cats and their wild cousins, the real fun begins. It's time to watch and play with your cat—and explore your wild sides.

Index